How-To
News Writer

*25 ways to develop
reporting and writing skills*

By Michael Bugeja, director
Greenlee School of Journalism and Communication
Iowa State University of Science and Technology

Greenlee School • Ames

Contents

Introduction and acknowledgements 3

1. How to recognize rights 5

2. How to adjust your attitude 7

3. How to spell 10

4. How to learn grammar and usage 12

5. How to edit copy 15

6. How to detect plagiarism 18

7. How to interview 21

8. How to dictate a story 23

9. How to attribute 24

10. How (and how *not*) to quote 28

11. How to write a lead 30

12. How to rewrite a lead 32

13. How to write a cutline 36

14. How to write a correction 37

15. How to handle fillers 38

16. How to use a futures file 39

17. How to spot and write a bright 40

18. How to cover and write about a speech 42

19. How to cover and write about a meeting 45

20. How to cover and write about crime and courts 47

21. How to cover a news conference 50

22. How to cover the legislature 51

23. How to find feature ideas 55

24. How to write a feature 58

25. How to create a code of ethics 60

Introduction and acknowledgements

This book is dedicated to the late Harry Heath, reporter for *Stars and Stripes* and longtime educator and defender of the First Amendment.

Heath earned his doctorate at Iowa State University of Science and Technology in 1956 and was a faculty member under Jim Schwartz, former chair of the journalism department (1965-77) and distinguished educator, in whose name ISU's Greenlee School of Journalism and Communication continues to honor journalists who have made significant contributions to the craft.

Harry Heath

Schwartz writes that Heath's lifelong contributions to journalism were substantial. "It was a privilege and delight to work and grow with him as he was trying his wings in the setting that he came to love: journalism education."

Heath left ISU to become the director of the Paul Miller School of Journalism and Broadcasting at Oklahoma State University. In 1979 he hired Michael Bugeja, author of *How-To News Writer* and current director of the Greenlee School, out of United Press International, where Bugeja was state editor for North and South Dakota. Heath inculcated in Bugeja a deep, abiding respect for the First Amendment, and together they worked for eight years as a team, visiting newsrooms in Oklahoma on annual grants from the Oklahoma Press Association.

In 1985 the association also funded the first edition of *How-To News Writer*, which helped thousands of aspiring journalists learn the craft in community newspapers in Oklahoma. The association graciously reverted rights to the handbook back to Bugeja in 2003 upon learning that he planned to dedicate the handbook to the memory of Heath.

The Iowa Newspaper Foundation agreed to republish the work via a $5,000 grant to the Greenlee School. The foundation and Bugeja will split royalties, with the foundation's share being funneled back into its work to support Iowa newspapers. Bugeja's royalties will be used for First Amendment scholarships for students at the Greenlee School. [*Note*: If you are interested in donating to that fund, send your check to 101A Hamilton Hall, Iowa State University, Ames, IA 50011, and mark on the check or in a letter: "To be used for Michael Bugeja's First Amendment Fund."]

Heath and Bugeja, using *How-To News Writer,* emphasized accuracy and ethics in their seminars, and the Oklahoma Press Association will create a CD of this handbook to further the cause, again in Heath's memory.

Schwartz understands Heath's enduring influence on Bugeja, who will pass that influence on to you in *How-To News Writer.*

Writes Schwartz: "Anyone fortunate enough to have worked with Harry Heath as a colleague and friend, as I was during his years on the journalism faculty at Iowa State University, knew from the start of his passion for accuracy and fairness. They were his hallmarks.

"Harry was an excellent teacher. His students respected and admired him for his dedication to the craft, for the breadth of knowledge he brought to the classroom and for his insistence upon professional performance.

"Above all, Harry was committed to preserving First Amendment freedoms. He well knew that the struggle to maintain and broaden the meaning of these rights is a battle that never is fully won, that eternal vigilance on the part of the people and the press is the only responsible posture."

How-To News Writer emphasizes basic skills, including accuracy and fairness, as part of that responsible posture. With craft and credibility, journalists empower the First Amendment and inform citizens of the Republic about the pertinent issues of the day.

1. How to recognize rights

*Congress shall make no law respecting an establishment of **religion**,*
or prohibiting the free exercise thereof; or abridging
*the **freedom of speech**, or of the **press**; or the right of the people*
*peaceably to **assemble**, and to **petition** the Government*
for a redress of grievances.
— The First Amendment to the U.S. Constitution

Journalists rely on the First Amendment to the Constitution, which has five parts. Memorize them. If you don't, you won't recognize them when you need them, and you need them every day.

To learn more about your rights, visit the Freedom Forum's Web site at www.freedomforum.org. The text below is reprinted with permission of the First Amendment Center, 2003.

Religion

The First Amendment prohibits government from establishing a religion and protects each person's right to practice (or not practice) any faith without government interference.

The Freedom Forum's First Amendment Center operates several Religious Freedom programs advancing the understanding of freedom of religion in public schools and other venues.

Free speech

The First Amendment says that people have the right to speak freely without government interference.

The First Amendment Center presents several programs addressing aspects of free speech, including Freedom Sings! and First Amendment on Campus.

Free press

The First Amendment gives the press the right to publish news, information and opinions without government interference. This also means people have the right to publish their own newspapers, newsletters, magazines, etc.

The First Amendment Center provides a program for newspaper editors and staff through a partnership with the American Press Institute.

Assembly

The First Amendment says that people have the right to gather in public to march, protest, demonstrate, carry signs and otherwise express their views in nonviolent ways. It also means people can join and associate with groups and organizations without interference.

Rights

Petition

The First Amendment says that people have the right to appeal to government in favor of or against policies that affect them or that they feel strongly about. This freedom includes the right to gather signatures in support of causes and to lobby legislative bodies for or against legislation.

2. How to adjust your attitude

Cub reporters and novice writers usually suffer the same symptoms: They read too little, dislike legwork, elevate style over substance, back into stories and advance their own interests.

They also misperceive the role and responsibility of editors.

Nothing new about that, of course. But the computerization of the newsroom has intensified these symptoms and misperceptions. Beginners think Lycos is legwork and e-mail, an interview.

Cyberspace is vast, so why write tightly?

These notions come at a bad time. Technology has downsized editorial staffs, especially at magazines, so fewer editors are available to mentor interns and recruits.

Beginners used to learn by experience, often with editors at their sides, adjusting attitudes.

That has to be done now in the classroom. If you aren't enrolled in journalism school, you need a how-to handbook.

Below are ordinary attitudes about the writing process, followed by adjusted ones. The writing process is just that, a series of steps. Journalists who take shortcuts usually stumble.

But the biggest stumbling block is mental.

Bad attitudes

Don't read other writers' work at your publication. Why show interest in anyone else's writing or waste time reading it? Use that energy to promote your own copy with editors and to admire your own published work.

Don't do research. Why bone up on your topic? Readers will remember your byline because of style, not substance.

Don't do interviews. Why talk to sources when you can be writing? The sooner you start, the sooner your byline will appear in print.

Don't abandon your "style." Why write according to tenets of objectivity or tone of voice? You'll end up sounding like every other writer in the newspaper or magazine.

Wow your editor by setting mood. Why reveal everything in the lead or introduction or explain terms, jargon or technical information? Better to hook readers with technique.

Don't analyze headlines in newspapers or compose titles for magazine pieces. That's the editor's job. Let them earn their pay.

Finish as soon as possible. Why give competitors the edge? Submit your work when you finish a draft that pleases you.

Don't worry about misspellings, grammar or length requirements. Why worry about typos and verb tense? Why count, cut and add words when doing so hampers creativity? As long as your words "flow," editors will be pleased.

Attitude

Adjusted attitudes

Dispelling the above myths is half the attitude adjustment. The rest is process and includes these steps:

Read the work of other writers. Reporters and professional writers are avid readers because they love words and facts, gemstones of journalism. They analyze quotations, paragraph structure, form, diction, length and more. They discern editorial standards: *How did this writer inform, enlighten or entertain readers? Is the story the right length for the topic? Should the writer follow up with a more detailed or edifying account?* And so on.

Research your piece. To write or report effectively, know as much as possible about the topic. You can also determine in advance whether editors will be interested in your idea. If they printed a piece similar to yours, read it to see whether you can add a new angle. Access databases and back issues to identify other published works on the topic. That will hone your idea so that it is more insightful or effective.

Invest in interviews. If you read and research, you will come across sources who can provide expert comment. Find contact numbers on the Web or in directories, and set up face-to-face or telephone interviews. The more sources you contact, the more you will know about your topic and the more reliable your piece will become in the process.

Use an appropriate voice. Think in terms of voice rather than style. Voice is the "sound" on the page or screen. Editors usually want an objective or authoritative tone for news but relax those standards with features or columns. You should be able to describe voice with a few adjectives—conversational, factual, witty, etc. Align tone with publication. Is your voice appropriate? If not, conceive another tone, or change the slant.

Ground your piece with a clear lead or introduction. Editors hate mood and call that backing into a story. Use opening paragraphs to convey what your story is about (topic). Then define terms and translate jargon and technical information and anything else potential readers might not immediately recognize or know. That helps clarity and readability.

Conceive a headline or title that foreshadows content. Analyze headlines in your newspaper or target market for style and tone of voice. True, editors often compose titles at newspapers or change them at magazines. Studying the relationship between headline and lead helps you compose better leads. Magazine writers compose titles to convey tone, topic and theme to editors, engaging them from the start.

Let your piece cool. You'll feel exhilarated simply because you finished a manuscript. That does not mean it is good. Resist the urge to send your work to editors the moment you complete it. Don't worry about competition. The easiest way to give competitors an edge is to send editors sloppy copy.

Polish your piece. Sharpen transitions. Excise padding. Use livelier verbs, more accurate nouns. Read copy aloud to sustain voice. Fix bad syntax. If you don't know how to spell, look words up. The same goes for grammar. As for length, remember that editors want it all—all the news that is fit to print *and* all the news that fits. Target specific sections. Count words of published work. Match that work.

That's the spirit.

Attitude really is everything. Those who adjust theirs impress editors. They muster the energy to do legwork. They set or maintain standards. They beat rivals the old-fashioned way, earning their stories and the readers' respect.

3. How to spell

Spelling

Journalism is a tough business. You can spend a week researching and writing a front-page article. Your editor is behind you all the way—paying mileage, expenses—anticipating a blockbuster of a story. And you deliver that story, an exclusive about a foreign trade deal that will pump dollars into your community. Throughout the article, though, you misspell a word: *foreign.*

The editor is fighting mad. "I should fire you," she says. "Numskull."

The reporter says, "I'm not stupid. The rule is *i* before *e* except after *c.*"

The reporter has a point. English is a difficult language with more than 800,000 words. He only misspelled one, and he relied on a rule that didn't apply. "Why the commotion?" he may ask. "Isn't it the editor's job to look up words?"

No.

The editor is right to cause a commotion. If reporters cannot spell the topics of their stories, why should readers believe anything else they write? Furthermore, the computer allows easy editing of copy, and reporters have to use this tool properly to save time and money. Really, there is no excuse.

Spelling is basic to good writing. So basic, in fact, that often we overlook it. When a misspelled word appears in print, however, it tarnishes the story. Cheapens it. Casts a bad light on the reporter and the product. Yet writers who cannot spell do not have an intellectual problem. *They have a muscular one.* They would rather take a chance on a near-spelling than reach for a bulky book and wade through pages to look up a simple word such as *foreign.* Oh, they will look up *carburetor* or *catalytic.* They know they cannot spell those. But they may not look up *receive* or *questionnaire.*

By the way, use a real dictionary—not a search engine or Web site. Some are reliable. Many are not. For instance, in 2004, the misspelled word *foriegn* was cited on 149,000 Web sites in a google.com search. All the Internet did was verify that *foreign* is often misspelled.

Reporters should realize there is a range of words they think they can spell—but cannot. To prove this, a study was done in the newsroom of *The Daily O'Collegian* at Oklahoma State University. The most commonly misspelled words were ones reporters were apt to use every day. *Receive* was misspelled an average of 10 times per month. Other top 10 words were *a lot, all right, renovate, innovative, caliber, aggressive, flier, integrate* and *commitment.*

So many factors cause us to misspell. For instance, the study showed that Oklahoma accents were responsible for these improper spellings: *jarnalism* for *journalism, reguardless* for *regardless, varify* for *verify, pance* for *pants* and *stomic* for *stomach.* The study also showed that reporters often use real words that sound right—but are wrong. *Examples:*

- The offices will be divided by *petitions.* (partitions)
- He intends to *alternate* the plan. (alter)
- He will *regulate* the panel. (moderate)

Of course, some misspellings were just plain dumb, as in *awhere* for *aware*. The editor in this case sang the student reporter a chorus of "Awhere, awhere has my little dog gone? Awhere, awhere can he be?"

To spell properly, be aware (not *awhere*) that common words can cause problems. The way you say a word may not be the way you spell it. Consult the dictionary or stylebook every time you question a word.

Be wary of spelling rules. English is a mixture of many languages. There are, for instance, 13 ways to spell the *sh* sound as in *show*, *mansion* and *chaperone*. Thus, for every rule there is an exception that, with your luck, will appear on the front page.

Worse, nobody in a newsroom wants to help you spell a word. You can ask the reporter across from you to spell a word. You can take a chance that the answer is the proper spelling for your story. Or you can do the dirty work yourself and look up a word in the dictionary.

If you cannot spell a word, some reporters ask, how do you look it up? One way is to think of a word that is similar in meaning, say *different* for *diverse*. If you can't spell *diverse*, look up the entry for *different*, and under synonyms you may find your word. Or look in a thesaurus under *different*. As a last resort—and I mean a last one!—telephone or e-mail your local library's help desk. Once an editor could not find the correct spelling for *bejabbers*, a word that can be pronounced *be-jeebers*. Because he seldom asked others how to spell a word, everyone in the office wanted to help him. But they didn't know what the slang term meant or how to begin to spell it. Rather than risk a misspelling, the editor telephoned the librarian, who had the answer at her fingertips.

Some reporters do not know how to use the dictionary. *Example:*

After reading this sentence—*Veterinarians are seeking many bazaar animals for experiments*—an editor asked a student journalist to look up *veterinarians* and *bizarre*. He came back righteously defending *bazaar*. He looked it up, and the spelling was exactly as he had it in the sentence. He looked it up, all right. *But he didn't read the definition.* Make sure you look up the correct word and do not confuse it with a homonym, a word that sounds like another but differs in meaning.

Also, hyphenated, compound and double words (such as *dog days*) are troublesome if you do not understand dictionary symbols. *Dog days* can appear as *dogdays* when you mistake the space between the words as a syllable indicator. *Dog • wood* can become *dog wood* or *dog-wood*, depending on whether you mistake the dot symbol for a space indicator or a hyphen.

The key to good spelling is attitude. If you were taking an open-book quiz in a math class and you needed the formula for the area of an isosceles triangle, chances are you would look it up. Journalism is a social science. Near-spellings do not count. When you don't know the spelling of a word, you have to overcome your muscular handicap, reach for the Webster and crack it open.

4. How to learn grammar and usage

Read handbooks on grammar and usage. Begin by mastering these common problems:

affect/effect   To solve the problem, you need to know the difference between a noun and a verb. *Affect* is a verb almost all of the time. *Effect* is a noun 90 percent of the time (ballpark figure). *Affect*, used as a noun, is an obscure psychological term. *Effect*, used as a verb, means "to cause" and also sounds awkward in a newspaper story. So the best rule is to use *affect* as a verb and *effect* as a noun, and you will have solved the problem.

who/whom   To check for proper usage, insert *he* every time you have used *who* in a clause. Insert *him* every time you have used *whom*. After you substitute *he* for *who* and *him* for *whom*, recast the clause into a sentence. *Examples:*

- Reporters consult with the newspaper adviser, who editors say always listens. CHECK: Editors say *he* always listens. *Who* is correct.
- Reporters consult with the newspaper adviser, whom they admire because he listens. CHECK: They admire *him* because he listens. *Whom* is correct.

which/that   Use of *which* adds to or helps clarify the term or phrase preceding it. That is why such a clause requires a comma before the word *which*. You can remove the clause without changing the meaning of the sentence. Use of *that* is more restrictive. It does not require a comma because a clause that uses *that* is essential to meaning. To check, remove the parenthetical clause from a sentence using *which*. The meaning should not change. (Parenthetical, by the way, means explanatory—like this sentence.) If you remove the clause and the sentence changes meaning, you should use *that* without a comma. *Examples:*

- This book, which sells for $14.99, helps fund First Amendment scholarships.
- This is the book that helps fund First Amendment scholarships.

it's/its   *It's* is a contraction; *its* a possessive pronoun. We add an apostrophe and *s* to form both the contraction and possessive of most nouns, as in *father's here* and *father's hat*, respectively. Thus, *it's* works like the typical contraction. (All third-person pronouns do.) *Its* does not work like the typical possessive. RULE: No possessive pronoun, even *its*, takes an apostrophe. *It's* always means "it is." ALTERNATIVE: Memorize it.

they're/their/there   Words that sound alike but have different meanings cause problems because they are hard to spot in copy. Worse, few rules apply to help you use them properly. To know the difference between any homonyms, even triple ones such as *ware/where/wear*, you have to memorize them. If you want an aid to memory, rhyme: *"grisly* fare for the *grizzly* bear." Rhyme: *"They're* on a dare in *their* underwear *there."*

disagreement Two types: noun-pronoun disagreement and noun-verb disagreement.

First type: We make the mistake in one direction, singular to plural, as in, "The Nebraska football *team* had *their* best offense ever in 1983." We wouldn't write, "The *Cornhuskers* had *its* best offense ever in 1983." CHECK: When you use *their*, make sure the antecedent (word it refers back to) is plural.

Second type: We make the mistake when the second of two nouns is singular and entices us—through sound—to use the singular tense, as in, "I do this, in part, because the writing and research *helps* me in the newsroom." The solution is the Jack and Jill rule. As soon as you spot the conjunction *and*, check whether it joins a compound subject. If so, you need the plural. Plug *Jack* and *Jill* into the sentence: "I do this, in part, because *Jack* and *Jill* help me in the newsroom." EXCEPTION: False plurals *every* and *each*, as in *"Each (Every)* writing and research assignment helps me in the classroom."

lie/lay Without *lie* we'd have as many problems with *lay-laid-laid* as we do with *win-won-won*. *Lay* takes an object: "Today I *lay* down *the book,* yesterday I *laid* down *the book,* I *had laid* down *the book." Lie* doesn't take an object: "Today I *lie* down, yesterday I *lay* down, I *had lain* down." *Lay* is the culprit, because it is the present tense of one word and the past tense of the other, the chief source of error. *RULE:* Memorize them. CHECK: When you use *lay* without an object, make sure you want the past tense of *lie/recline*.

active/passive Somewhere, sometime, some English teacher has told you to always use the active voice. True, you tighten language through it: "He took the cake" is better than "The cake was taken by him." It's more specific: "A chef baked and decorated the cake" is better than "The cake was baked and decorated." But the passive voice exists for a reason, and the rule is when the object of a sentence is significantly more important than the subject, use the passive voice: "JFK was killed by an assassin's bullet." When you employ the active voice in such cases—"An assassin's bullet killed JFK"—the writing sounds forced.

conciseness Ernest Hemingway, who wrote features for newspapers before he published books, once said that good writing was 90 percent nouns and verbs. You can tighten your writing by choosing exact nouns and verbs and eliminating unneeded adjectives and adverbs. Adjectives weaken nouns. They indicate that the writer could not think of a better word. Don't write "the gold and white horse" if you mean "palomino." Don't settle for "a bright red color" if you mean "crimson." Some adverbs can be deleted immediately: *very, rather, quite, some-*

what. Adverbs weaken verbs and indicate poor diction. Don't write, "The man *walked* slowly into the room" when he *sidled* or *lumbered* into it. Good writing habits come with practice. Writers who fail to tighten their language and who disregard proper grammar and usage in their articles have no business working for newspapers.

Grammar

5. How to edit copy

Copyediting is paramount in a point-and-click era as print and new media vie for readers with shorter attention spans.

Most editors and writers know the basic rules:

One word rather than two to express the same idea: *thump* instead of *strike dully.*

Active over passive voice: "The editor thumped the desk, rejecting another manuscript" instead of "Another manuscript was rejected by the editor, who struck the desk dully."

Nouns and verbs over adjectives and adverbs: "Editors dislike wordiness" instead of "Typically, wordiness is not appreciated by bleary-eyed editors. ..."

You get the point.

Let's sharpen it by shunning, when possible:

Extreme mood setting: "John Doe slumps down in his chair until midnight amid the slush and stale pizza in front of piles of unsolicited manuscripts threatening to avalanche across his half-empty bottle of cola and onto the grimy tile floor of the newsroom at *The Quill*."

"To be" constructions: "*There are* many reasons why Doe rejects submissions, and wordiness is one of them."

Conjunctive constructions: "There are many reasons why Doe rejects submissions, *and* wordiness is one of them."

"To be" appositives: "Doe, *who is* editor, dislikes wordiness in manuscripts."

Excessive possessive constructions: "There are a lot *of* reasons why Doe, who is editor *of The Quill*, dislikes wordiness, and length *of* articles is one *of* them, because *of* availability *of* space in the magazine."

Exclamatory comments: "Editors dislike wordiness. Less is *really* more!"

Parenthetical comments: "Editors dislike wordiness because magazine space is precious *(depending on which section of the book a writer is targeting, of course)*."

Rhetorical comments: "Editors dislike wordiness. *Why shouldn't they?*"

Unprocessed quotations: "Too many writers and reporters tend to be wordy. True, freelance writing should be conversational or at least pronounceable. It shouldn't ramble. We just don't have the space. Good prose—good magazine prose, at least—plants an image or idea in the mind of the reader, phrase after phrase," Doe said.

Unprocessed research: "According to Doe's internal audit on unsolicited manuscripts, approximately one filler submission out of 69 per month is accepted, along with one out of 43 articles and one out of 57 features, requiring 14 hours evaluation of snail submissions and 12 hours of e-mail submissions per staff person per week during the magazine period ending Jan. 1, 2000."

Adverbial time elements: *"Before* taking a sip of his soda pop, Doe rejects another query *after* reading his umpteenth submission and noting the perils of publishing *today."*

Adverbial transitions: *"Consequently*, it is tougher than you might think to publish a padded manuscript. *However*, a freelancer's chances of success will improve by using copyediting techniques. *Otherwise*, you will waste time and money and give up on the dream of being a published writer."

Avoiding these pitfalls is effective, often able to halve word length.

You can use these techniques to polish your prose, fill holes efficiently or focus on design. You'll also appreciate editors, especially if you're trying to work with or sell work to one.

Compare versions

Unedited: 268 words

John Doe slumps down in his chair until midnight amid the slush and stale pizza in front of piles of unsolicited manuscripts threatening to avalanche on his half-empty bottle of cola onto the grimy tile floor of the newsroom at *The Quill*.

There are many reasons why Doe, who is editor, rejects submissions, and length of articles is one of them, because of availability of space in the magazine.

Editors dislike wordiness. Why shouldn't they? Less is really more (depending on which section of the book a writer is targeting, of course).

"Too many writers and reporters tend to be wordy. True, freelance writing should be conversational or at least pronounceable. It shouldn't ramble. We just don't have the space. Good prose—good magazine prose, at least—plants an image or idea in the mind of the reader, phrase after phrase," Doe says.

According to Doe's internal audit on unsolicited manuscripts, approximately one filler submission out of 69 per month is accepted, along with one out of 43 articles and one out of 57 features, requiring 14 hours evaluation of snail submissions and 12 hours of e-mail submissions per staff person per week during the magazine period ending Jan. 1, 2003.

Before taking a sip of his soda pop, Doe rejects another query after reading his umpteenth submission and noting the perils of publishing today.

Consequently, it is tougher than you might think to publish a padded manuscript. However, a freelancer's chances of success will improve by using copyediting techniques. Otherwise, you will waste time and money and give up on the dream of being a published writer.

Edited: 112 words

Editor John Doe sulks amid slush and pizza, sipping cola and reading manuscripts until midnight.

He dislikes wordiness because of length requirements.

Good magazine prose should plant an image or idea in the reader's mind, phrase after phrase. "It shouldn't ramble," he says. "We just don't have the space."

On average Doe and staff spend 26 hours per week per person reading manuscripts, accepting only one each of every 69 fillers, 57 features and 43 articles.

Doe reads his umpteenth submission, still sipping pop, and rejects another query, noting the perils of publishing.

Learn how to tighten your prose and publish more by using copyediting techniques. Save time, money and your dream.

Editing

6. How to detect plagiarism

Reporters who suspect someone has plagiarized a story have an ethical obligation to report that to their editors. Editors have a legal responsibility to detect plagiarism.

Plagiarism is a firing offense in most newsrooms.

Before you accuse a reporter or writer of plagiarism, you must have evidence. Suspicion is not enough. Never accuse someone of plagiarism without that evidence, or you can expose yourself and your newspaper to countercharges or even legal action.

Step 1: How to distinguish plagiarism from similar concepts

Definition

Plagiarism is stealing or closely imitating someone else's written, creative, electronic, photographed, taped, promotional or research work, identifying it as your own. The original work is called the *source document*. The plagiarized work is called the *target document*. [*Note:* Plagiarism also can entail technicalities such as citing a book at length without proper attribution in each paragraph.]

Legal vs. ethical considerations

Intent is associated with plagiarism. It helps distinguish between legal and ethical infractions. In other words, a person can commit plagiarism without intending to do so—and still can be held responsible by the person who created the original work. That's the legal consequence. Intent is, however, a factor in ethical considerations, because making a choice to steal is a moral decision reflecting a person's value system.

Plausible deniability involves justifying one's actions by using an excuse that relies on viewpoint or mindset, which a third party can never fully know. Plausible deniability is a common defense used to circumvent moral responsibility.

Paper-era excuse of "coincidence." Before the advent of electronic publishing, when most plagiarists changed wording or paraphrased, plausible deniability typically involved coincidence to explain away similarities between source and target documents. As wording between such documents was similar but not exact, coincidence may have been a suspicious but plausible excuse in the absence of hard evidence.

Internet-era excuse of "ignorance." Because most plagiarism cases now involve the Internet, where source documents are readily available and easily copied, coincidence no longer is a factor. The chances of randomly selecting identical wording—even for one paragraph—are literally astronomical. So plausible deniability has shifted from coincidence to ignorance. When a reporter says, "Geez, I didn't know copying stuff from the Internet was wrong," that excuse involves ignorance. A person who claims not to

Plagiarism

have known that copying someone else's work off the Web was wrong may or may not be telling the truth. One can always make that suspicious but plausible excuse—*even in the presence of hard evidence*.

Challenging the ignorance defense. Some claims of ignorance may be true. These usually involve inappropriate footnoting. Few, if any, plagiarists invoke the coincidence defense anymore. While ignorance may be a plausible excuse for plagiarism, it is not so for the concept of *conscience*, which indicates one's value system. Ignorance is closely associated with the concept of negligence—whether a journalist *should have known* that the actions were wrong. Negligence, as a legal concept, typically invites swift and severe consequences.

Concepts often confused with plagiarism

Copyright infringement involves using a substantial portion of a document or reprinting research findings or statistics, images and data from software or computer programs without the originator's permission. [*Note:* Plagiarism may or may not infringe on copyright, depending on the portion in question. Infringement is adjudicated on a case-by-case basis. As a rule reporters typically limit their selections—with attribution, by the way—to no more 200 words from any book and no more than 5 percent from any article. Permission is always sought to reprint poetry or music lyrics.]

Proxy plagiarism, or *reverse plagiarism*, involves the creation of an original work with the intent of allowing another party to pass it off as his or her own. Examples are many but include doing a report for another person out of friendship or profit; writing or producing a news story or video for another person's byline; adding a scholar's name to a submission without his or her knowledge or contribution, simply to increase chances of acceptance; or generating research in someone else's name, with or without permission, to gain favor or reward.

Matching story, often mistaken for plagiarism, entails using someone else's news or feature story as a template to generate a *match*—or competing story. This is done ethically by adding new research and conducting interviews. *Never use research or quotations from another story in your match*. Do not "borrow" quotations from a competitor's story and make them indirect, either. When you match a story, do not use a byline or pretend to be in another city by using a false dateline—known as a *magic carpet ride* in the business.

Invention entails fabricating portions of or an entire document, quotations, source names and histories, or research findings or statistics. The content is passed off as true when, in reality, it is fictitious. [*Note:* The motive is not to program media but to circumvent the legwork or labor involved in generating a news or feature story.]

Hoax, a specific type of invention by a person or group, involves making or disseminating a false claim with the intent to program or manipulate the news media for personal gain, exposure or some other motive. [*Note:* Hoaxes include e-mail, hate messages, damaging claims, allegations and news purported to come from a person or group when, in actuality, they are fabrications meant to manipulate or generate outcomes.]

Step 2: How to gather evidence

Search via engines. Thanks to the Internet, you have access to dozens of search engines to track down source documents. Here are some popular ones: Google, Excite, Alta Vista, Yahoo!, Lycos, et al. If one search engine fails, try another. You can also use a meta-search engine such as www.metacrawler.com, which accesses multiple search engines. To learn more about search engines, check out Search Engine Watch at www.searchenginewatch.com.

Start with the first paragraph. Your word thief probably stole from the top of the source document. So enter into a search engine a phrase from the first paragraph. There's another reason to start with leads: Many search engines, publication archives and library databases summarize them in abbreviated listings.

Choose awkward or odd phrases. If your search fails using leads, enter awkward locutions into a search or meta-search engine. An Ohio University student was caught plagiarizing because she used British spellings and these odd-sounding phrases in a final project: "indispensable guarantors" and "considering advertising's social impact." In less than 10 seconds, a meta-search engine generated addresses for five sites containing the source document.

Use unlikely word combinations. The word *Boolean* means logical word combinations, such as "advertising AND ethics." A few years ago that combination produced 14,774 hits on Excite.com — far too many to weed through in your hunt for a source document. To catch a plagiarist, make your Boolean searches with unlikely combinations, taking a rare word from the plagiarized document — *beanbag*, for instance — and combining that with your operative word. By contrast, the combination "beanbag AND ethics" yielded 13 hits on Excite.com.

Use library databanks. Boolean searches are perfect if you are searching library databanks — most of which now are online. Databanks often supplement information that search engines omit. Typically, though, you won't be able to access the source document but an abstract thereof, which should provide you with enough information to decide whether you should access an article from an online newspaper or magazine.

Access specific archives. Boolean searches work exceptionally well with magazine and newspaper archives that feature online search options. Some Internet publications require subscriptions before allowing access to archives; others charge a fee per downloaded article. Either way, it can be a good investment.

7. How to interview

The mistake is so common there is a cliché for it: *going into an interview empty-handed*. This occurs when beginning writers conduct interviews without having done the necessary research, when they ad-lib questions and fail to follow up, and when they waste time by requesting simple information.

Before you prepare questions, you must decide which organizations, professions and people need to be interviewed. Reporters who research subjects and sources occasionally know nearly as much as the experts they interview. The strategy has many benefits:

- The source will be impressed with the reporter's knowledge
- The source will be less able to dodge questions.
- The reporter will be able to anticipate questions and ask intelligent follow-ups.
- The reporter will be able to express jargon in common language.
- The source and reporter will spend more time discussing important matters and less time clarifying terms or noting information easily obtained in advance from a résumé.

The résumé or background of a source is especially important. It contains such information as past jobs, honors and awards, publications and personal data such as age, children, health, etc. When you arrange an interview, you should request a résumé or locate one online or in the library if your source is well-known. Check references such as *Who's Who* or more specific directories that contain bibliographic data, such as *The Directory of American Poets and Fictions Writers*. If your source works for a corporation or institution, the personnel or public relations department might be able to supply you with background sheets not available online.

If you need to learn about the subject of your interview—say, center-pivot irrigation systems—visit your public library in person or online. In addition, request information from manufacturers or from dealers. You might find additional material at an agency such as a county Extension office or the U.S. Department of Agriculture. In short, always consult the library and then contact anybody else associated with the subject. By doing so, you not only will learn more about your subject but will learn about people whom you later may want to interview.

After you have studied a subject or source, prepare a list of names, addresses and telephone numbers of all people you intend to interview. You should keep your lists in a computer file, of course. But you also want to print the list and keep it by your telephone so you can contact your sources or return messages quickly. Make the necessary appointments, preferably at places where the sources feel comfortable, such as their homes or offices. Once this is done, you may start preparing your questions.

Interviews

In the notepad you will take to the interview, jot down one question per page. Toward the bottom of each page, write "follow-up" in case you need to clarify or acquire more information. Base your questions upon research, never whim, and keep in mind that there are two types of questions: one that elicits a specific response and another that elicits a general response—known as closed-ended and open-ended questions.

Closed-ended questions usually can be answered in one or two words. Often, they elicit a yes-no response, of little use in an article. But sometimes they produce the perfect answer for your story. *Example:*

> *Writer:* "Which football player did you come here to recruit?"
> *Scout:* "James Spencer."

Open-ended questions usually require the source to speak at length about a subject or person. They provide the responses that you will highlight as direct quotes in your story. *Example:*

> *Writer:* "Why does your team want to recruit linebackers?"
> *Scout:* "The average age of our starters is 33, and we're looking to rebuild. If we don't sign rookies like James Spencer, we're likely to run into trouble next season."

When a closed-ended question fails, employ a series of open-ended questions that lead to a closed-ended one. *Example:*

> *Writer:* "Which football player did you come here to recruit?"
> *Scout:* "I can't answer that."
> *Writer:* "What do you look for in an athlete?"
> *Scout:* "Speed, agility, intelligence—any talent that helps a player get the job done."
> *Writer:* "Do you think Iowa State players have such talents?"
> *Scout:* "Not many, at least not the caliber that a guy needs to play professional football. But I like a player or two."
> *Writer:* "Speed, agility, intelligence—which ISU player has all three?"
> *Scout:* "James Spencer."

Finally, when interviewing a source for your article, be sure to absorb your surroundings. Telephone interviews are better than e-mail ones—avoid those, if possible. But both are less effective than personal interviews. You can view facial expression, for instance. Also, how people decorate their homes or clutter their home offices can tell you more about personality than the best résumés.

8. How to dictate a story

Spell out proper nouns, using common words to indicate letters that might be distorted over the telephone. *Example:*

Written: Bugeja
Dictated: B *as in boy*, U, G *as in George*, E *as in Edith*, J, A *as in apple*.

Indicate all punctuation. *Example:*

Written: "He was the first to be killed," she said.
Dictated: Quote He was the first to be killed *comma end quote* she said *period*

Indicate all printing instructions. *Example:*

Written: The man was a Marine. He was the first "casualty."
Dictated: The man was a Marine *uppercase period continue graph* He was the first *quote* casualty *period end quote end graph begin new graph*

Combined example:

Written: "The man was a Marine. He was the first 'casualty,'" Bugeja said.
Dictated: Quote The man was Marine *uppercase period continue quote* He was the first *single quote* casualty *comma single quote end quote* Bugeja B *as in boy*, U, G *as in George*, E *as in Edith*, J, A *as in apple* said *period end graph begin new graph*

(If the above quote ends the story, final instructions will be: *period end graph end story.*)

9. How to attribute

Nobody sees the word *said*. When you use it in a sentence, readers skip right over it. That is why the word is so important. When you use another word to replace *said*, you stop readers. You make them focus on attribution instead of information.

Of course, you can use this to your advantage. When a source says something that may not be fact, such a word as *contended*, *alleged* or *maintained* makes the reader focus on the attribution. In this case, replacing *said* enhances objectivity. Here are some tips to help you attribute:

Tense

Use past tense when you attribute. Some feature stories begin well with the present tense. However, you must sustain that tense throughout the entire story. If you begin a feature with *says* and find yourself using *said* in the body of the story, recast the beginning to conform to the past tense.

Placement

Put a person's title and name before *said*. *Examples:*

• Mayor John Smith said, "I am proud of my past and will run for re-election."
• "I am proud of my past and will run for re-election," Mayor John Smith said.

If a person's title is more than two words, you may put *said* before the name and title. But you should use it at the end of the sentence. *Example:*

• "I will run a clean campaign and win," said Jane Doe, juvenile court judge.

Place the attribution at the beginning, at the end or at a natural break in the sentence. *Examples:*

• The mayor said, "If I see her tomorrow, I will press charges."
• "If I see her tomorrow, I will press charges," the mayor said.
• "If I see her tomorrow," the mayor said, "I will press charges."

Introduction of sources

When you introduce the first source in your story, it does not matter whether the name precedes or follows the quotation. *Examples:*

• "I will press charges," Mayor John Smith said.
• Mayor John Smith said, "I will press charges."

However, when you attribute a second source in your story, the name must precede the quotation. When you neglect to do this, you may cause confusion, as in these paragraphs:

> "If I see her tomorrow, I will press charges and see that she is imprisoned for obstructing justice," Mayor John Smith said.
>
> "I am tired of all the senseless lawsuits filed by politicians trying to be re-elected," Judge Jane Doe said in reference to the mayor's threat.

(If the judge's name preceded the quotation, the reader would have been certain who was speaking in the second paragraph.)

Explanatory material

Explanatory material inside direct quotations should be one or two words enclosed in parentheses. Do not insert the definite article *the* or the indefinite articles *a* or *an*. If you use more than two words, consider making the quotation partial or indirect. *Examples:*

> • "Everyone has a right to it (freedom of expression). I intend to continue speaking out against the mayor," Doe said.
> • Everyone has a right to freedom of expression, Doe said. "I intend to continue speaking out against the mayor."

Paragraphing

Only one attribution is needed for a paragraph of two or more sentences of direct quotation. *Example:*

> "I will not buckle under threats by a mayor who puts himself above the law," Doe said. "He hasn't even apologized for using tax money to pay for campaign literature."

If you want to continue the above quotation in a separate paragraph but without another attribution, drop the ending quotation marks in the preceding paragraph. *Example:*

> "I will not buckle under the threats by a mayor who puts himself above the law," Doe said. "He hasn't even apologized for using tax money to pay for campaign literature.
>
> "The time to apologize is over. If he had any integrity, he would drop out of the race."

However, if you close the quotation at the end of a paragraph and then want to continue the quote to a new paragraph, you need another attribution. *Example:*

> "I will not buckle under the threats by a mayor who puts himself above the law," Doe said. "He hasn't even apologized for using tax money to pay for campaign literature."
>
> "The time to apologize is over. If he had any integrity, he would drop out of the race," Doe said.

Attribution

Finally, you cannot continue a partial quotation in the same manner as a complete one. When you use a partial one, you need to close off the quotation and use another attribution in the subsequent paragraph. *Example:*

> Doe said the mayor "hasn't even apologized for using tax money to pay for campaign literature."
> "The time to apologize is over," she said.

Partial quotes

Use them sparingly. They often seem out of context or mislead the reader. If you use a partial quote, ask yourself why you cannot use a complete one or why you cannot simply make the quotation indirect. *Examples:*

> *Partial*: Doe contended the mayor had made "a mockery" out of the bidding system because he contracted with friends.
> *Complete*: "The mayor contracts with friends who submit bids to the city," Doe contended. "He has made a mockery out of that system."
> *Indirect*: By contracting with friends who do business with the city, the mayor has made a mockery out of the bidding system, Doe contended.

In the above case, the indirect quote or complete one would be the best choice. The partial quote leaves the reader wondering in what context Doe used the word "mockery."

When you use a partial quote, make sure the verb agrees with the subject without changing the quoted words.

> *Wrong*: No matter how often the campaign falters, the mayor "intends to run for re-election and win." (For this quote to be correct technically, the mayor had to say, "I intends to run for re-election and win.")
> *Right*: No matter how often the campaign falters, the mayor intends "to run for re-election and win."

Partial quotes are practical sometimes for the lead of an important story. When you highlight an exciting word or phrase in the lead, however, you must repeat the full quotation in the body of the story. This way, you show the reader that you did not quote a source out of context. *Example:*

> *Lead*: The mayor has made a "mockery" out of the bidding system by contracting with friends, contended Judge Jane Doe, who has vowed to defeat incumbent John Smith in the November elections.
> *Fourth paragraph:* "The mayor contracts with friends who submit bids to the city," Doe contended. "He has made a mockery out of that system."

Tampering

Most editors do not allow reporters to tamper—or change—what a source says within direct quotations. If a source uses bad grammar, the reporter uses an indirect quote to remedy the problem. Some editors allow small changes to fix grammar or usage within a direct quotation. However, keep in mind that the direct quotation is a basic contract. When readers see quotation marks, they assume the words were said verbatim. Your newspaper will lose credibility if you tamper with direct quotations.

Attribution

10. How (and how *not*) to quote

Quoting a person accurately is one of the most sacred rules of journalism. When you put quotation marks around words and attribute them to a source, you are telling the reader that those words were actually spoken in front of you.

Fabricating dialogue may be legitimate in fiction or public relations (as long as the practitioner clears the quote with the client or source). In journalism, however, quote-making is called invention.

And it's taboo.

Because of e-mail and the Internet, many writers are becoming lax about the sanctity of direct quotations. Dialogue these days passes as chat, typed on keyboards rather than spoken and transmitted electronically anywhere on the globe.

Before home computers, most writers felt obliged to inform readers that a quote was said "in a telephone interview." Otherwise, they feared, the audience would incorrectly assume that the quotation was made face-to-face.

Fewer writers are making these fine distinctions—much to the concern of editors in newsrooms across the country.

"I feel the sanctity of quotations is absolute," said Peter Copeland, editor and general manager of Scripps Howard News Service, which prides itself on accurate, well-honed feature stories for subscribers.

"Readers have the expectation that things in direct quotations are 'preserved under glass'—that they have a special place in the text," Copeland added in a telephone interview from the Scripps-Howard newsroom in Washington, D.C.

Magazine writers must uphold the same standard, he said.

You can do that by learning the don'ts, do's, and maybes of direct quotations:

Don't invent quotations. Your job is to put your sources on record—not to put words into their mouths. If a source refuses or is unable to give you the quote that you need, go back for another interview or go to another source.

Don't lift quotations from other stories. The Internet makes it easy to locate sources with nifty things to say. If they didn't say those things to you, you can't pass them off as your own—or even verify that the quotations are authentic.

Don't excerpt passages and cast them as quotations. You can access all kinds of documents online, including speeches, court proceedings, testimonials and minutes of meetings. You can cite them as such. But you can't reprint them as quotations, pretending that the source said the excerpt to you in an interview.

Do research sources on the Internet before interviewing them. Everything from résumés to public records is available online. Accessing information before interviews saves time and earns respect from your sources because you did the necessary legwork. You won't ask basic questions such as "What do you do for a living?" or "What lawsuit, in particular, are you challenging again?"

Do interviews face-to-face when possible. Good journalism writing relies on sensory data, descriptive passages that appeal to the five senses or convey emotion. You can't always convey that doing telephone interviews, which may suffice for a quick, expert quotation but seldom for a biography or an article.

Do process interviews to avoid long direct quotations. The risk of doing telephone interviews is that your prose may sound more like a transcript than a story. If you do research in advance of your interview and question your source face-to-face, you will process quotations naturally, making some indirect (or paraphrased), adding necessary description and maintaining your voice—the sound that readers hear on the page.

Maybe you can correct grammar and syntax. Purists will argue that you can't fix such common errors as wrong verb tense or idiom, noun-pronoun disagreement and run-on sentences. When you get such quotes, purists believe, you should make them indirect. Realists believe you can make minor corrections that typically involve a word or two. Your goal is to quote sources, realists say, not embarrass them. BOTTOM LINE: If you change meaning when you change a word, you can't use a direct quotation.

Maybe you can do e-mail interviews. Purists argue that e-mail is typed, not spoken, and lets sources invent their own quotations rather than participate in spontaneous exchanges with the writer. Thus, purists claim, e-mail interviews are bogus. Realists believe that e-mail is speech and more accurate. Better still, writers have transcripts when sources deny that they said something. BOTTOM LINE: When you use an e-mail interview, note it as such in the attribution.

Maybe you can let sources see their quotations in advance. Purists argue that your job is to quote sources accurately—not to ensure that they are comfortable with what they said. Realists believe that writers sometimes misquote sources, especially when information is technical. BOTTOM LINE: If you let your sources see their quotations in advance of publication, advise them that they cannot change meaning—only inform you of any mistakes.

How you quote sources reflects your standards, especially in an electronic age when emphasis is on convenience rather than legwork. If you take shortcuts with quotations, you can lose more than assignments.

You can lose your reputation.

Quotes

11. How to write a lead

A beginning writer would never say to a spouse or friend what is written in the typical lead. Often the beginner overwrites, becoming ensnared in long, complex sentences that contain "highfalutin'" words. Consider this lead written by a first-year journalism student about the repeal of a local beer ordinance:

- Because of decreased concern on behalf of town leaders in litter caused by discarded beer cups, voters seemed willing to do away with the local beer ordinance.

Students would never say that to their roommates. Instead, they would proclaim: "You can drink beer in the streets now and not get arrested" or "The beer ordinance has been repealed." Either of those remarks would be a better lead than the one above.

Beginning reporters tend to overwrite because they lack confidence. Maybe they remember the cadence of network news and think they have to use it to make their stories sound professional. The overwritten beer-ordinance lead above has a network cadence. Before the student composed his poor lead, he may have heard one like this:

- Despite continued threats of terrorism by leftist rebels in El Salvador, officials announced today that elections to name a new president would proceed as planned.

Beginners lack the verbal skills to make such a lead click. They would be better off clearing the journalese from their heads and writing a "roommate" lead.

After you have interviewed a source and returned to the newsroom, you should psych up for your lead. Pretend your story is as vital as a news bulletin. Imagine your roommate, friend or spouse, and say what first comes to mind. That is usually the most important aspect of your story. Then write it down. *Example*:

- I just spoke with a doctor who told me that too many Iowans are fat. Being fat is unhealthy, she said. Iowans used to die of old age, but now more are dying of things such as heart attack and stroke.

Now circle essential words; *doctor, Iowans, fat, unhealthy, old age, dying, heart attack, stroke*. String them together in a sentence.

- Too many Iowans are fat and unhealthy, no longer dying from old age but from heart attacks and strokes, a doctor said.

Look at your notes to see whether you can add anything to the lead. In this case, we might want to establish the credentials of the doctor, ending the lead with "said Dr. Jane Jones, state health director."

There are other approaches. Some writers psych themselves up to write and then just type the first thing that comes to mind. They type everything they can remember about a source or subject, just to get going, hoping that sooner or later a lead will come. If you decide to try this method, remember the need for rewriting is the strongest here. Don't be fooled by a false sense of completion that marks the end of any creative project. Cut poor phrasing, and tighten your writing.

Some reporters employ a notebook method. When a source says something that might make a good lead, they jot down "L1" next to the quote. If they hear another good lead, they mark "L2," "L3," etc. When they are ready to write, they refer to these quotations and base their leads on the best.

Others resist the temptation to write, mulling over the facts they can remember, running through a dozen leads in their heads. When they begin writing, the words—finally released—flow to the page. This is a method that requires a good memory and one that takes longer to master.

Whatever your approach, remember that the lead should be a promise of what is to come in your story. Don't hook your readers on false promises. *Example*:

• Iowans are eating so much these days—and dying because of it— that soon nobody will be around to do the cooking, a doctor says.

Apart from being clever, this lead exaggerates fact and fails to set the proper tone for the doctor's warning. Reporters have a pact with their readers. They do not fool them; they gain their trust, and they keep their interest by writing the best possible stories.

Leads

12. How to rewrite a lead

Put the news first

Example: The Iowa Department of Revenue and Finance has recommended that the Legislature increase the state sales tax by a penny to offset anticipated budget shortfalls.

Problem: Proper nouns, especially agency names, bore readers. Bury them.

Method: Place the newsworthy clause before the proper noun that begins the sentence.

Rewrite: Legislators should increase the state sales tax by a penny to offset anticipated budget shortfalls, the Iowa Department of Revenue and Finance has recommended.

Combine sharp sentences

Example: "The Fishing Magician," "Mr. Bass," "Clayton Douglass." All three descriptions are one in the same.

Problem: Feature writers have to sell the subject of their stories quickly and creatively. They cannot afford to back into the lead.

Method: If the writer appears to back into the lead, resist the urge to create a new top and scan the second through fifth paragraphs. Usually you will find sentences to combine for a lead.

Rewrite: If he isn't the finest fisherman in Clear Lake, he's as close as anyone to claiming the title—not bad for a man who just recently got hooked on the sport.

Avoid second-person question leads

Example: What do you do if one day the federal government tells you it intends to confiscate the land your family has farmed for five generations so it can build a lake?

Problem: The question begs a silly answer. "You bury toxic waste in your fields." The reader anticipates a punch line, which eliminates the element of surprise. The writer is forced to switch from the second person to the third person in the body of the story.

Method: Combine the best elements of the question and the punch line. Keep the lead in the third person.

Rewrite: When the government evicted Bill Chitwood to build a lake on land his family farmed for five generations, he went to court—not to keep the acreage but to haggle for a price.

Junk the jaded lead

Example: Well, it's done. At a special meeting Friday, city commissioners approved the final version of the 2003-04 fiscal year budget.

Problem: If a writer is bored with a topic, why should a reader find interest in it?

Method: Read the entire story. Circle pertinent facts. Combine those facts for a lead.

Rewrite: Some part-time airport employees now can count on full-time work and some city department heads on merit raises, thanks to the new city budget approved Friday.

Mend the mixed metaphor

Example: There were 11 requests to drill oil wells before the planning commission Thursday night, each hoping to eventually sprout a gusher but instead all dying on the vine.

Problem: Derricks spout, not sprout (carrots do). Grapes and gossip (not oil wells) die on the vine.

Method: If you must use metaphor to create your lead, be consistent. Use words in keeping with the idea you are trying to put forth.

Rewrite: Drillers hoping their wells would spout gushers made 11 requests for permits Tuesday, but each bid came up dry.

Eliminate easy quotation leads

Example: "Most people quit or say, 'That's good enough.'" Not Jack Jones, a writer who believes in persistence and dedication. "You've got to pay your dues," he says. And he has—more than 200 rejections before his first best-seller.

Problem: Few sources say things better than writers can phrase them.

Method: The typical quotation lead indicates that the source impressed the writer. Look to direct quotations to provide phrases for your lead.

Rewrite: Author Jack Jones collected more than 200 rejection slips, but he believed in paying his dues. And the strategy has paid off—in millions.

Slay the say-nothing lead

Example: The reorganization of the telephone company has caused some interesting rate changes in long-distance calling.

Problem: This type of lead promises much but delivers little, usually only the topic of your story.

Method: To test whether you have a say-nothing lead, read the first paragraph aloud as a broadcaster might, and then stop. A say-nothing lead will sound humorous, because it is woeful lying incomplete. Scan the second through fifth paragraphs for lead material.

Rewrite: The best times to call long distance are listed by the telephone company in the current directory, but since the recent reorganization, this and other charges have been changed.

Shun the one-word lead

Example: Violence. A problem that affects nearly 20 percent of dating couples, said Kathleen McKay, a sociologist.

Problem: Writing one-word leads is easy because the reader does most of the work, imagining the range of possible meanings. Typically, such a lead produces another fragment that the reader must splice for meaning.

Method: Make the fragment that follows the one-word lead an appositive, and look to the second through fifth paragraphs for more material to complete the lead.

Rewrite: Violence, a problem that affects nearly 20 percent of dating couples, ranges from shouting to rape, said Kathleen McKay, a sociologist.

Don't define

Example: The American Agricultural Movement is an organization of hundreds of family farmers who want to have a say in U.S. farm policy.

Problem: A sales representative would not make a pitch by defining the product—"A vacuum is a device to clean carpets"—and neither should the writer. The typical definition is as exciting as a dictionary. Worse, it belittles the reader because it begins at square one and withholds information.

Rewrite: Farmers who recently returned from a protest in Washington are bouncing atop tractors again at harvest, but woe to the politician who tries to take them for a ride.

Ditch the background lead

Example: Vocational Education Week, Feb. 12-18, is being recognized by the three vo-tech facilities that serve county students.

Problem: This lead is really a background paragraph, information that is timely and factual but too weak to sustain an article.

Method: Look to the second through fifth paragraphs for lead material. Make the background lead your second paragraph.

Rewrite: Students who do poorly in the classroom but work well with their hands often gain confidence in their potential at area vo-tech schools, county educators say.

Vocational Education Week, Feb. 12-18, is being recognized by the three area vo-tech facilities.

Abandon the crutch

Example: An Ames man was killed Monday five miles west of Boone when a car left the eastbound lane of U.S. Highway 30 before colliding head-on with a semi-trailer truck, authorities said.

Problem: Crutch words such as *when, after, before, following, as, during,* and *while* make all types of news leads sound similar because they impose the same structure on the sentence. Abandoning the crutch forces the reporter to write concisely.

Method: Cast elements of a crutch lead into chronological order and rewrite

Fixing leads

concisely.

Rewrite: An eastbound car collided head-on with a semi-trailer truck on Monday, killing an Ames man five miles west of Boone on U.S. Highway 30, authorities said.

Add the final touch

Example: Earthen scars concealing 10 miles of new waterline now snake through Laurens community northeast of Storm Lake. Creeping along, it sidles up and bumps to a stop at the house where Sarah Flynn lives with her daughter's family.

Problem. Sometimes a reporter writes creative leads so well that he, she or the copy editor takes them for granted and forgets about final touches. In the example above, an earthen scar cannot snake, creep, sidle and bump without mixing metaphors. Also there is subject-pronoun disagreement.

Method: The writing, not the writer's reputation, counts. Don't ease up when you see the byline. No matter how polished a lead may appear to be, re-read it for subtle errors.

Rewrite: An earthen scar concealing 10 miles of new waterline snakes through Laurens community northeast of Storm Lake. It coils to a stop at the house where Sarah Flynn lives with her daughter's family.

Fixing leads

13. How to write a cutline

Read the reporter's entire story, not just the lead. That will give you an overall idea of the story's newsworthiness. You also may spot an interesting fact or statement that enhances a particular photo's newsworthiness.

Scan your contact sheet or digital file for photos that communicate *more* information than the story does. Remember, a picture is worth a thousand words. If that is true, a picture should enhance a story's newsworthiness by at least a fraction of that thousand.

Readers should be able to associate the photo and the story without a cutline. For instance, a story about a gasoline shortage and a long line of cars at a gas station are immediately linked as cause and effect. A story about that shortage with a picture of a lollipop-licking toddler in the back seat of a car waiting to gas up may be enticing and cute, but readers would have difficulty seeing the connection between shortage and lollipop and toddler.

Use a tagline, if appropriate, to enhance connectedness between photo and story. A tagline, or mini headline for a photo, uses one or two words that link photo and story. Those words should not simply repeat the obvious, like "car crash," but should highlight a news element, like "no seatbelt."

Your cutline should be brief—usually no more than a sentence or two—and be just as focused, concise, factual and gripping as any news lead. It should:

- Contain correct spelling and grammar, especially of names, sites and proper nouns.
- Include accurate information depicting the scene or identifying the event or source.
- Use phrases that focus on fact and enhance newsworthiness—again, don't repeat the obvious.
- Rely on strong nouns and verbs. Circle nouns and verbs in the cutline. List them on a piece of paper. They should tell a story. If not, use stronger nouns and verbs.
- Avoid stereotyping, libeling or offending the audience by being cute, satirical, inaccurate or profane. (The annals are full of journalists who wrote fake cutlines as jokes that somehow got into the newspaper.)
- Emphasize symbol and/or irony in the photo, if evident. *Example:* In a feature about a female race-car driver who took up and succeeded in the sport, there is irony in the tagline and cutline:

Victory Lane

First-place finisher Lane Smith is kissed by her boyfriend, mechanic John Doe, at a pit stop—showcasing how far she has traveled from NASCAR fan to winner's circle.

Cutlines

14. How to write a correction

Nobody's perfect, especially the reporter for a newspaper. Readers know this. In fact, when readers know something personally about a story—the homemaker who scans a column about cooking, the farmer who follows a series about irrigation—chances are they will find inaccuracies. The best policy then is to admit errors and place corrections prominently in the newspaper. When you do this, you enhance the credibility of your publication.

Only in two cases should you consider not running a correction. If a source or attorney threatens a lawsuit because of an inaccuracy, the printing of a retraction can be used as evidence that a libel has been committed. When this occurs, notify your publisher and newspaper lawyer immediately. Also, when a minor error occurs, you may not want to bother with a correction. For instance, you may report that a new high school basketball coach is 43 when she actually is 44. Some editors will argue that a formal correction for a mistake of this magnitude is a waste of space.

Some guidelines to observe in writing a correction:

Make it as brief as possible. One paragraph is standard.

Tell when and what happened. "Friday the *Iowa State Daily* incorrectly identified Government of the Student Body President John Doe in a cutline under a picture of Hamilton Hall. Likewise, information about the renovation of Hamilton Hall contained information about Doe's graduation plans."

Tell how it happened, if appropriate: "This occurred when cutlines for the two pictures inadvertently were switched."

Apologize. "The *Daily* regrets the error."

Corrections

15. How to handle fillers

Fillers are short articles, usually between one and three paragraphs. Editors need them to fill holes on a page. Fillers should be evergreen—a shelf life of at least one month—and prepared in advance so that the copy desk has a ready supply.

Do not subscribe to filler services. The typical service sells trivia, such as "camel facts" or "pizza consumption per year." Fillers may be smaller than most news articles, but you should treat them with equal respect. Here are some sources:

The wire service. Ask the wire editor to route all unused wire stories to a reporter assigned on a slow day to write fillers. The reporter should choose evergreen stories—features, for example—and condense them to make newsworthy fillers.

PR releases. Ask section editors to save all news releases that they would normally discard. Although some of these may be poorly written, you may find enough information for a filler. The practice also helps promote good relations with the community.

Historical facts. Use important dates such as Dec. 7, 1941, when Pearl Harbor was attacked; Nov. 22, 1963, when President John F. Kennedy was assassinated; or Sept. 11, 2001, when the World Trade Center and Pentagon were attacked. Consult back issues of your newspaper to see what occurred locally. How did your community respond?

Library. If your section is entertainment, consult the appropriate reference books in the library to write fillers about rock 'n' roll or celebrities. If your section is sports, you can locate native athletes who are listed in national directories. Whatever reference book you choose, be sure to cite the edition in your filler. *Example*: "Will Rogers, who began his stage career with a lasso act spiced with a bit of humor, earned the nickname 'Cowboy Philosopher' during those vaudeville days, according to the *Dictionary of Biography*."

Leftover notes. The editor should ask reporters to prepare fillers from unused portions of their notes. What cannot be used in a story often can be salvaged for a filler.

Résumés. Request résumés from civic leaders, faculty and teachers, judges and even clergy. You will be surprised at the accomplishments that make good filler material.

16. How to use a futures file

Use a box or container large enough to store your file folders. A loose-leaf notebook with tabs to separate the days also works.

Number folders (or sheets of cardboard or paper) from 1 to 31, each number representing a day in any month.

Before you file an idea for an assignment, mark it with a start-up date or other instructions so that you know when you must begin and complete your work. (If you use paper or cardboard, file ideas *in front* of the numbered sheets.)

Staple or paperclip any literature, research or supporting information to your written and marked assignment.

At the start of each day, pull the appropriate file.

[*Note:* You can use computers to do this, but the problem concerns storage of clippings and other documents. You can scan those into a file, of course; but that is too time-intensive.]

A futures file

PHOTOS BY SHAUNA STEPHENSON

Michael Bugeja shows Greenlee School students how to use a futures file.

Futures

17. How to spot and write a bright

A bright, also known as a brightener, is a short human-interest piece that enhances any page in the newspaper. When a bright appears on the front page, screened or attractively bordered, it becomes an element of design. It entertains and attracts readers. Often the use of brights is the difference between a mediocre and a lively newspaper.

Unfortunately, they are hard to come by and even harder to write.

A bright is often an odd or off-beat story that, at first glance, has little news value. For instance, while covering the legislature, you might meet a tourist who shows you a brochure during lunch at the cafeteria. The tourist, from Germany, is confused because the brochure promotes the statehouse as a seventh wonder of the world. The fellow feels a little cheated. You can share a laugh at the hype. Or you can ask him a few questions for a bright.

This actually happened to a reporter at the *Lincoln Journal-Star*, and this is what he wrote:

> LINCOLN, Neb. — Josef Auer, 25, Munich, Germany, was baffled after reading in a Nebraska travel brochure that the statehouse was billed as a seventh wonder of the world.
>
> "I just couldn't believe it," he said. "It looks like a small skyscraper from New York, with a mosque on its top."
>
> Mary Goebel, tourism coordinator at the Capitol, said the 412-foot-high structure—designed by Bertram Goodhue of New York and completed in 1932—ranked one of the seven wonders "by a *Reader's Digest* poll of architects in the early 1940s."
>
> "I'm not sure of the other six, but I know the statehouse was rated above the Cathedral of Notre Dame and the Taj Mahal," she said.
>
> Auer, currently touring Nebraska before starting graduate school in Manchester, England, said he plans to travel across the state "in search of more Nebraska wonders."

Occasionally, a news release or filler can become a bright with a little leg-work. You have to train yourself to see the extraordinary in the commonplace. For instance, this news release became a bright with a little more information and a lot more creativity:

> Tom Reddy, a 22-year-old truck driver, will be one of a dozen young men entering the University of South Dakota in August to become a registered nurse.
>
> Until the academic year begins, Reddy will continue to work for Fire in the Lake trucking company. Upon completion of the two-year program, he will study at a hospital to become a nurse anesthetist.

To write a bright from such a news release, you have to focus on the lead. It has to sparkle like a poem. After all, you want to entertain your readers with believe-it-or-not copy. The best way to do that is hook them at the start.

In the first few paragraphs, don't be afraid to turn a phrase. But know that unless you turn it well, the phrase will turn on you and nobody will believe what you write.

After a punchy lead and lively informational paragraphs, follow with a good direct quote that takes the reader into the story. Add more information, and then end with a summary paragraph that is factual and adds credibility to your topic. *Example:*

> MECKLING, S.D. – At the helm of an 18-wheel, Titan 90 semi-truck is a bearded South Dakotan who hauls hay across the Midwest and wants to be a nurse.
>
> Tom Reddy, 22, of Vermillion, trucks in Nebraska, Iowa, Minnesota and South Dakota but soon will trade his dusty overalls for hospital whites.
>
> He has enrolled in the nursing program at the University of South Dakota, in hopes of becoming a nurse anesthetist.
>
> "I want to become a nurse because it's a good way to deal with people," he said. "I also like the lifestyle. You don't have to work 12 hours a day like a doctor."
>
> Reddy, known by his fellow truckers as "the Ever-Reddy Roller," says his co-workers for the most part have accepted his career choice.
>
> "Their first reaction is to gawk. But when I explain why I want to be a nurse, they usually say, 'Right On!'"
>
> Until the academic year begins, Reddy plans to keep trucking for Fire in the Lake Co. He will be one of dozen young men entering the University of South Dakota to become registered nurses. Upon completion of the two-year program, he will study at a hospital to become a nurse anesthetist.

The above bright took time and effort to write, but it probably was the most-read item that day on the front page.

When you gear up to write such an article, remember this:

Keep it short.
Keep it light.
Keep it punchy.
That's a bright.

Brights

18. How to cover and write about a speech

Step 1: Covering a speech

The assignment

Your editor receives a letter, an e-mail or a news release informing the newspaper that a speech is planned. The editor assigns the story to you.

The advance

An advance is an article of a few paragraphs that tells when and where the speech will be delivered. It helps build reader interest.

Rewriting the PR release

PR writers will try to get their company and product names before the public—free publicity. So usually you will need to rewrite releases to stress what is newsworthy.

Original:

STILLWATER – The Chamber of Commerce proudly announces that John Doe, president of Domestic Steel, has consented to give a speech titled "A Pox on Lexus" at 7:30 p.m. Thursday at the Chamber of Commerce Building.

Mr. Doe says foreign luxury cars seem like good buys because many experts believe they are put together better and are more reliable, but Americans may be paying more than they bargain for if they consider the higher insurance rates they will have to pay for certain models and the effect on the American economy. Mr. Doe has many interesting and varied things to tell us.

The Chamber invites interested citizens to hear this important talk. As usual, cookies and punch will be served free of charge.

Rewrite:

STILLWATER – Foreign luxury cars, heralded for their workmanship and reliability, may not be the best buy for an American's dollar, according to John Doe, president of Domestic Steel.

Doe is scheduled to give a speech at 7:30 p.m. Thursday at the Chamber of Commerce. A Chamber spokesman said Doe's talk, "A Pox on Lexus," will cover a wide range of topics, from higher insurance rates for foreign luxury cars to their impact on the U.S. economy.

After the speech, refreshments will be served.

Arranging coverage

After you write the advance, telephone the organization or group sponsoring the event. Request materials on the topic and speaker. See whether you can arrange an advance interview or receive an advance text of the speech.

Research

Look up the topic or facts about the speaker in a reference book or trusted online source, or telephone local experts for comment. For the speech in question about Lexus, you would check blue books to see whether foreign cars have higher resale values than American models. You also would interview local car dealers.

The interview

After your research, prepare questions to ask the speaker. *Example:*

• What can you tell Americans who know that foreign cars have higher resale values?
• How do you account for the claim that foreign luxury cars require less service and lower maintenance costs than models by U.S. competitors?

If possible, ask such questions before the speech so that you can return quickly to the newsroom. If you are on a deadline, you can beat the competition. If you are not on deadline, you can start on another project, sidebar or assignment.

The speech

If you have an advance text, follow it word for word and note any changes, deviations or ad-libs. The text now becomes a source for direct quotations. If you do not have an advance text, record the talk or take traditional notes, preferably both.

Check-in

When you arrive in the newsroom, before you begin writing, tell your editor if anything extraordinary happened (so the editor gets an idea of where to place your article). Explain, too, how many inches of copy you anticipate writing (so the editor gets an idea of how much space to give your article).

Speeches

Step 2: Writing a speech story

The lead

The first paragraph introduces the topic and something significant about it, along with an attribution from the speaker. *Example:*

> An American who pays the cost of a foreign luxury car may not realize that a neighbor may be footing the bill, John Doe, president of Domestic Steel, told a Chamber of Commerce audience Thursday night.

The bridge

Use a good direct quotation for the second paragraph. The quotation should support or help clarify the lead. *Example*:

> "The Lexus in your garage may be good on gas, but we in the steel industry are running on empty," Doe said.

The body

Use the inverted pyramid, from the most important facts and quotations to the least important. Alternate with direct or indirect quotes, research, comments from other sources and, finally, circumstantial details such as information from a résumé or vita.

The sidebar

If appropriate, write a sidebar—a related story, smaller in size and significance—to accompany to main story. *Example:*

> John Doe captivated local residents by putting "a pox on their Lexus" to help the U.S. economy, but nobody expected him to leave town in a Mercedes-Benz.
>
> "This is embarrassing," Doe said, when asked about the $54,000, German-built car. "I actually own a Mercury Cougar, but my company supplies executives with luxury vehicles."
>
> Doe, president of Domestic Steel, was the featured speaker Thursday at the Chamber of Commerce. He advised the audience to trade luxury foreign cars for American models and revitalize the economy.

19. How to cover and write about a meeting

Step 1: Covering a meeting

Meetings and public hearings are tough assignments. Typically they are conducted informally. A reporter has to know in advance how a session will proceed. Parliamentary procedures will be followed in a formal meeting, such as a city council session. But the reporter has to lay the groundwork to cover informal meetings of task forces and advisory committees. Here's how:

• Arrive early and ask someone in charge whether people who testify will sign a sheet of paper with their full names and addresses. If not, request it. This will help you identify witnesses who appear before a panel.
• Find out the exact problem or topic under consideration.
• Get plenty of quotations from panel members and witnesses.
• As the meeting progresses, use cue symbols (for example, stars or check marks) in your pad for quotations or information that you will have to clarify or attribute.
• After the meeting, ask panel members about the next step. Were members satisfied with the testimony? evidence? findings? When will the report or decision be made public? Are more hearings planned? If so, where and when?

What to do if you are barred from a meeting or denied access to records
Government meetings should be open to the public. A reporter is the public's representative. Records should be public, too. If you are barred from a meeting or if someone denies you a public record, contact your state's Freedom of Information council. To learn more about your rights and open meetings, visit the National Freedom of Information Coalition Web site at www.nfoic.org/.

The mission of the coalition is aligned with the learning objectives of *How-To News Writer*:

"The National FOI Coalition joins First Amendment and open government organizations from individual states in a self-supporting alliance as they seek to protect the public's right to know through the education of media professionals, attorneys, academics, students and the general public. NFOIC nurtures start-up FOI organizations in other states. It assists its own members through joint fund raising, project planning and the interchange of ideas and information."

You also should contact your state FOI council and request a handbook. A list of addresses and contact personnel of local councils is online at the national coalition's site at this link: www.nfoic.org/Members.html.

Meetings

Step 2: Writing a meeting story

The lead

Start with an indirect quotation that shows action taken or interesting testimony. *Example:*

> Sewers will have to be repaired immediately, or Sioux City will face a multimillion-dollar problem within two years, a task force has determined.

The bridge

Follow with your best direct quotation. *Example:*

> "Taxes will triple in two years if we don't do something soon about sewers," panel member John Smith said.

The body

Alternate with direct and indirect quotations from panel members and witnesses.

The conclusions

End with secondary matter (minor business or action) for the public record. *Example:*

> In other business, the panel:
> • Installed a new secretary, Jane Webster of Hinton.
> • Voted to fund the Parks Department picnic at the same level as last year, $1,500.
> • Tabled a measure on the purchase of parking meters until revenue is determined and vendors identified.

Meetings

20. How to cover and write about crime and courts

Step 1: Covering crime and courts

Take time to understand the court process. Some reporters do not understand what the word *arrest* means (held for questioning). If authorities suspect a person may have committed a crime, they take the suspect to police headquarters and *book* him or her on the suspected offense.

Even if you have access to the police log, you might not want to identify the booked suspect. Some editors prefer that you wait until the official *charge*. That happens when the district attorney or, in some jurisdictions, a grand jury reviews the evidence and determines whether the prosecution should pursue the case. At that time a charge will be filed or the case dismissed.

If charges are filed, the suspect is *arraigned*—or brought before a judge. If the suspect has worked out a deal with the prosecutor, the judge looks over the agreement and informs the suspect of his or her rights and the consequences of accepting the deal. If the suspect pleads innocent, the judge sets bail, if any, and schedules a *preliminary* or *pretrial hearing*.

The suspect is now officially a *defendant*.

At such a preliminary hearing, the judge listens to evidence from the district attorney and defense lawyer to determine whether sufficient evidence exists to suggest that a crime may have been committed. Note how conditional all this is. In America, defendants are presumed innocent until proved guilty.

They have other rights, too. The Sixth Amendment to the Constitution reads, in part: "In all criminal prosecutions, the accused shall enjoy the right to a speedy and public trial, by an impartial jury of the State and district wherein the crime shall have been committed. ...."

The defendant also has the right to be fully informed about the "nature and cause of the accusation," according to the Sixth Amendment, and to be assigned legal counsel and confront witnesses during the court process.

Part of that process entails being *bound over for trial*. That happens when the judge at a preliminary hearing determines that sufficient evidence does exist against the defendant. The case is put on the district court docket. A jury will be selected (or jury trial waived by the defendant).

That's when "television drama" kicks in, and most reporters understand the process from there, following the trial with a jury of peers or judge determining the defendant's guilt or innocence. Thereafter, the appeals process can extend through the federal courts to the U.S. Supreme Court.

Of course, the courts determine other cases beyond crime. Those involve civil actions such as one neighbor suing another because of an accident in the home or a consumer (or many, in a *class-action* suit) suing a corporation because of negligence. The scope and range of possible legal actions are beyond this handbook, but you will become familiar with them by attending trials and by working with sources in the courthouse.

Courts

Step 2: Writing about crime and courts.

Visit the court clerk to determine what new cases have been added to the docket. Or go online and view those public records. If you do not understand a case in question, telephone the clerk for an explanation.

Contact the district attorney and defense lawyer for comment.

Cover the case from arrest to appeal using your futures file. (See Chapter 16.) This ensures that you will inform the public responsibly and regularly. You'll also generate dozens of stories as the case wends its way through the judicial process.

The lead informs the public of the latest news. *Examples:*

A local resident is being held in the May 8 beating and rape of a first-year student attending a Des Moines vocational school, police reported Monday.

Charges against the suspect are pending.

[*Note*: Always use *in* rather than *for* when writing about crime. If a suspect is arrested *for* a crime, it sounds as if he or she committed it. Also, in sexual assault stories, be sure to consult with your newspaper's ethics code to determine how to handle names of complainants. If your newspaper prohibits the identification of sexual assault victims, do not define the complainant in a way that compromises that identity.]

John Doe, local accountant, has been charged with felonious sexual assault in the May 8 beating and rape of a first-year student attending a Des Moines vocational school, the district attorney's office announced Monday.

In the body of the story, insert quotes from the police, district attorney, defense lawyer and any witnesses, using the inverted pyramid structure, with facts and quotations in descending order of importance.

Be sure to note the next step in the judicial process in a background paragraph recounting the history of the case:

The student was walking home from a party when assaulted in the alley behind her apartment, police said. She suffered injuries to her head and abdomen and was hospitalized overnight and released. Doe, who lives in the same apartment complex, will be arraigned June 20 in Polk County District Court.

In news about crime or courts, your reader should be able to stop after reading the background paragraph and understand the latest and most pertinent aspects of the case.

John Doe, local accountant, pleaded innocent at his arraignment Friday and was ordered held on $200,000 bond in the beating and rape of a first-year student attending a Des Moines vocational school.

Doe appeared before District Judge Thomas Smith, who set an Aug. 3 preliminary hearing.

"We will fight the charge," Jane Jones, defense attorney, said after the arraignment. "John is a respected member of this community and has never received a speeding ticket, let alone been accused of a crime."

Linda Miller, assistant district attorney, said police found pictures of the student in Doe's apartment, in addition to other physical evidence linking him to the crime.

Miller refused to discuss that evidence, to be presented at Doe's preliminary hearing.

On May 8 the student was walking home from a party when assaulted in the alley behind her apartment, police said. She suffered injuries to her head and abdomen and was hospitalized overnight and released.

Courts

21. How to cover a news conference

Before

Don't count on special seating unless your newspaper has arranged for it. The first reaction is to sit in the first row. But this may not be the best position if you need to leave quickly for deadline or if you have to use a pay telephone or cell phone. The front rows also may not be best to size audience reaction. Decide what seat best serves your purpose and deadline.

During

You need to listen and record answers to pertinent questions asked by other reporters. Ego sometimes gets in the way. If you are too eager to ask your prepared questions, chances are you will miss a good quotation. Also, be sure to get the speaker's response to a question by your competition. This will guarantee that your article will have as much information as your rival's.

Don't count on being able to ask two questions. When called upon, you can inform the speaker that you have more than one question. (Never exceed two questions. The speaker may advise you in front of everyone to arrange an interview through a press aide and then call on the next reporter.)

An easy way to ask two questions is to tack on "and I would like to follow up." *Example:* "What are the chances that the city manger will resign his post because of the investigation, and I would like to follow up."

After

Do not rush away from a news conference unless your deadline is crucial. You may want to procure documents from press aides and ask them for clarification or even to supply a missing word or two.

22. How to cover the legislature

Several months a year—in some places, all year or every other year—the state legislature will be in session. If you work in a capital city or if your editor sends you to the capitol on assignment, you need to know about the legislative process.

How do laws evolve?

A beginner may say bills are passed by the legislature and signed into laws by the governor. Essentially, that is true. The process, however, is more complex.

In a typical legislature, also known in some states as an assembly, a bill proposing a new law is drafted by a legislator or sponsored by one for a resident or group. Resolutions also are drafted but do not have the power of law and only put the state on record for or against issues.

Sometimes legislators need help interpreting existing laws so they can draft bills to conform to state statutes. The legislators consult the legislature's research council or other state drafting agency providing the service. Once drawn to specifications, the bills or resolutions may be pre-filed and given identifying numbers, such as Senate Bill 001 or SB001. House Bill 001 may be abbreviated HB001; Senate Resolution 001, SR001; House Resolution 001, HR001; Joint Resolution 001, JR001, and so on. Reporters should check to see what bills have been pre-filed and thereby get a beat on an important piece of legislation.

When the legislature is in session, the speakers or leaders of the house and senate will send the pre-filed bills to committee, where resolutions also are considered. In some legislatures, particularly Nebraska's, the procedure may be slightly different. Nebraska has a unicameral, or one-house, system in which every lawmaker is a senator. Still, bills in the Cornhusker State make their way to committee before action is taken upon the floor.

A senate bill on busing, for example, may be sent to a senate urban affairs committee while a house measure on increased property taxes may be sent to a house revenue committee. Be sure you know which committee will consider a proposal, because the house and senate each may have a revenue or urban affairs committee.

Much of this information is online at your legislature's Web site. For a list of state legislatures online, including information on pending legislation and other useful information, visit the National Conference of State Legislatures' site at www.ncsl.org/.

Before a bill is approved, amended, tabled or killed in committee, witnesses will be called to testify on the measure. If a committee approves a bill, it will be advanced to the house or senate for floor debate. Do not write that the committee *passed* the measure, because at this point it is still a proposal or unborn law.

A bill is shelved indefinitely if it is tabled. This means the committee may not consider the bill at all or may give it a low priority. Do not think that bill is

Legislature

dead, however. Immediate attempts may be made to bring the bill *off the table*. To do this, the committee first has to agree to untable the measure. A compromise amendment may be tacked at this time to the bill to increase the chances of it being sent to the floor. The committee must vote on the amendment and, if approved, then on the bill. The vote order is important if you use it in a story. A common error is to record the vote on the amendment, thinking the panel has approved the bill, when in fact the panel has only approved a change in the bill.

Even if a committee approves such a change, it still may table the bill again or kill it now. When this occurs, politics are usually involved. A politician may want an excuse for constituents on both sides of an issue. The legislator can tell those who favor a bill that the measure could not be supported *as amended*. The legislator also can tell those who are against a bill that, indeed, it needed to be killed.

Even if a bill is killed in committee, it later may be *smoked out,* or resurrected, during the floor debate.

In general, a committee may do these to a proposal:

• Approve it.
• Approve it with amendments.
• Hold it over until a specific day to allow absentee legislators, for example, to testify.
• Table it indefinitely.
• Table it until the day *after* the legislature adjourns, in effect killing it.
• Kill it.
• Not consider it.

Committees can get tangled in the legislative process, sometimes on purpose. Lawmaker No. 1 may propose an amendment. Lawmaker No. 2 then may make a motion to amend the amendment. The committee may agree to the *motion* and not to the amendment of the amendment. After agreeing to the motion, the committee votes on lawmaker No. 2's proposal. The committee may reject that. Then it must return to the original amendment by lawmaker No. 1. It may approve that, and then kill the bill for political reasons—after wasting 20 pages of your notebook.

House bills that make it out of committee are sent to the house floor for debate. The same procedure is followed senateside. The house and senate leaders give one or several days' notice to legislators before a bill is discussed.

You may follow debate from a press box near the action or from the gallery if your newspaper is a weekly or if you are unable to claim a box seat.

If party leaders allow, try to attend the daily caucus. In many ways, two-party politics resemble a football game. The caucus is the huddle. During strategic sessions, leaders map out tactics to be employed during committee or floor debate. Here are some "plays":

A *smokeout.* A legislator makes a motion to bring a tabled or killed measure out of committee to the floor for debate. To do this, he or she usually will need two-thirds of colleagues to agree. This occurs when one party has a majority in committee and the other party has a majority on the floor.

A hog house (slang in some Midwestern legislatures). A legislator stands up to promote an insignificant bill, one that enlarges the legal size of coyote traps, for instance. Twenty seconds into the speech, another lawmaker jumps up with a motion: "Strike everything after the enacting clause and add the following ..." The motion, subject to various rules, totally replaces the coyote trap bill, if approved. The tactic is used especially in South Dakota to revive bills that have been killed in committee. It also may be used if a legislator has missed the deadline for filing new bills.

Reconsideration. If a bill narrowly misses approval, a motion for reconsideration may be made to give the bill another shot on another day. This tactic is used if some lawmakers are absent during the vote or if sponsors feel they can lobby effectively during the interim.

Stalling. Certain legislatures have rules to delay a bill if an amendment is added to a measure. This is supposed to allow everyone time to understand the effect of the amendment. It may be used, however, to delay a vote so critics can lobby against the measure.

Once an approved bill leaves the house, it starts from the beginning senate-side, and vice versa. The leader assigns it to a committee. The measure is acted upon there and perhaps advanced to the floor for debate. Should the other chamber approve the measure without any changes, it goes to the governor for signature. If amendments are approved, it goes to the originating chamber for *concurrence* or agreement of the changes. The house may not agree with senate amendments, or vice versa, so a committee is formed with representatives from both sides. This is called a *conference* committee, which usually works out a compromise. Members of such a panel are called house and senate *conferees*.

After all this, the governor may veto the bill. Then it is returned to the house and senate for an *override* vote. Sometimes both chambers let the veto stand. But if they choose to override, generally two-thirds of each chamber much agree or else the veto is *sustained*.

Briefly, there is another way to make laws. It is initiative referendum legislation, or a version of the giant town meeting. Voters may decide a law passed by the legislature is wrong, or they may want to pass a law that legislators are avoiding, such as pari-mutuel betting or a state lottery.

Petitions for the new law are circulated; signatures are gathered and later sent to the secretary of state, who may pass them to county clerks. The clerks certify through voter registration that the signatures are valid and return the petitions to the secretary of state for a tally. If enough signatures appear on petitions, the issue is placed before voters. The people then elect to pass or reject the state question.

Whatever the issue, legislative copy does not have to be dull. Keep your objectivity, but try to convey the excitement of politics. Above all, be informa-

Legislature

tive. In the third or fourth paragraph of a legislative story, remember to tell the readers at what stage a measure is in the legislative process. If the house has approved a bill, for example, mention that the senate has yet to act on the measure.

Some writing tips:

- Translate political jargon.
- Write features about political personalities or their tactics.
- Research important issues affecting your state, and quote government officials on how they think a piece of legislation will correct or worsen a problem.
- Conduct surveys of legislators on how they will vote on an important bill, such as one calling for a tax increase.

You can find more stories in the legislature than you can possibly write. Hours are long, deadlines tough and the session seemingly endless.

One reporter told me, "Just when you think the session is over, you start preparing for the next."

Legislature

23. How to find feature ideas

Personal experience
Jot down the "facts" of your life, the highs and lows and turning points that color your background. Some highs: births, adoptions, accomplishments. Some lows: deaths, divorces, diseases. Turning points: religion, relocation, lifestyle. If you have been divorced, for instance, you may have dealt with attorneys, judges, counselors, social workers, clergy, family and friends. There are sources that accompany a system. You know the crucial issues. Brainstorm now for an idea.

The five senses
As you go about your daily routine, use your five senses to come up with feature ideas. You will be surprised at what you can overhear, see or otherwise sense. Once at a Lawton, Okla., hotel before an Oklahoma Press Association workshop, a reporter overheard a group of soldiers in the cafeteria discussing a secret assignment to Europe. That could have been a national story. It happens more often than you think— in *your* neighborhood.

The sixth sense
Feature writers should be able to spot fads before they happen. The best writers relate those fads to trends. A fad is short-lived, like the Pokémon craze of the 1990s. A trend endures, like card collecting. Combine the elements for the larger picture. Remember, the death of a fad is as important as its birth. People want to know what's in, what's out and why.

Localized stories
Look to the networks, newspapers and news magazines. Many of their articles, especially roundup stories, have local angles for feature stories. If *Time* does a national roundup on a shortage of flu vaccines, contact local medical sources to generate a good feature for your newspaper. Don't forget to include a paragraph up high that discusses the national problem. This gives your feature impact and substance.

The follow-up
Go through your newspaper's library or read back issues for annual, five-, 10-, and 20-year anniversaries of important events. What begins as a simple follow-up can re-emerge as a major feature, especially if nobody has bothered to check on developments.

Classified ads
Reporters hate to hear it, but many people buy newspapers to read the classified ads. Readers learn who is hiring, selling and getting personal. If a local factory places a classified for a dozen welders, you may end up with a story about

Ideas

a new contract that will pump dollars into your community. The Edsel or Packard up for auction can put you into contact with antique car enthusiasts. A notice to adopt a newborn can result in a feature about the process. When you base a feature on a classified ad, you can be sure of one thing: You are writing about a topic that has reader interest. Now add some news values and heighten that interest.

Directories

Let your fingers do the walking in the most common of all directories, the Yellow Pages. On the average, I can find one feature idea for every five entries. You read such an entry as "Abortion Information and Services" and then brainstorm for an angle that might interest your readers. Government directories can be used the same way. And don't forget the best source for profiles, *Who's Who*.

Trade publications

Feature ideas can hide in bland places. Trade publications, house organs and newsletters contain a wealth of information. You may have to suffer through stale prose, but chances are you will uncover a fresh idea. Remember that these publications are written for narrow audiences. Keep your reader in mind when adapting the subject matter.

Annual reports

A wealth of information is contained in annual reports filed by charities, corporations, trade associations, educational institutions and other organizations. Routinely request them, and keep a library in the newsroom or in your home office. The reports will tell you about profits, reorganizations, strategic plans and other vital developments. The publications also usually contain a list of contact personnel. Contact one to set up interviews, or set up interviews with personnel profiled in the reports.

Statistics

Once you find a good table or chart—even a figure—putting together a feature becomes a snap. Do not focus on the agency reporting the statistics, but on the people the statistics affect. For instance, if a state agency reports more crime and unemployment, do a feature on the people affected by crime and the economy. The government has stats on everything and everybody. You simply need to contact the right agency for a table or chart.

Research and medical journals

The reading here is slow, but most of these publications have a Research in Brief section that may include innovative work from an area scientist or physician. Interview that person, of course, but once more: Don't forget the people affected by the invention or treatment. Your feature will have greater value because of human interest.

Online databases

Databases online exist for almost any topic. When you decide on a topic—cancer treatment, say—you should visit a search engine and input the words, with proper quotations as indicated below:

"cancer treatment" and "online databases"

That Boolean search combination yielded 414 sites via google.com in 2004. You can wade through databases for specific topics—from research trials to genetic therapies, in the above case. That will help you conjure a number of specific feature ideas, perhaps for a series.

In general, when using online databases, rely on ones with *edu*, *org* or *gov* extensions to help ascertain whether the information is reliable. When in doubt, telephone your librarian or an expert in the field (in the above case, an oncologist, perhaps) and ask about the site in question and what other sites may be more accurate and reliable.

Ideas

24. How to write a feature

Features come in various styles and flavors. But the basic feature, or enterprise piece, is shaped like an hourglass. The lead has to hook the reader and introduce the subject matter in a personal way. Then you follow with a few informational paragraphs and the best direct quotation high in story and proceed with less important facts and quotes until about the middle of your piece. At this time, pivot the story toward a conclusion. Introduce facts and quotes that build—sentence by sentence—toward a powerful ending. The last paragraph of your story should be the "second lead." It should not simply recap or state the obvious but impress the reader beyond expectation.

A good approach is to create a feature based on a news event. When you do this, you add real-life drama and make your story more effective. Can a story about a barn fire in South Dakota be newsworthy enough to be transmitted nationwide by an international wire service? It depends. No, if the writer composes the typical inverted pyramid stating simply that the barn was destroyed by fire and X-number of livestock were killed. Yes, if the writer depicts the news so that the readers feel the same emotion as the participants in the event. A national wire service ran such a barn story because the reporter focused on a fire that killed the farmer's livestock and destroyed pets and machinery. Put yourself in the farmer's situation: His livelihood, his family dogs, his son's Christmas presents, his pride-and-joy of a barn—all were lost one winter night when his wife noticed that smoke, not snow, was blowing off the barn roof. This is human interest that relates to any reader anywhere.

Tragedy strikes without warning. Readers know this. The New Yorker may not own a barn but will imagine the pain of losing pets, presents and property. That is the power of a feature.

You may find it difficult to convey human interest in an event that is largely visual, such as a parade. A television crew would have no trouble covering a parade, but a writer would. To do it well, the writer would have to rely on the ability to describe the scene so that readers felt they had witnessed this event. This is a *color* feature.

Note the difference between the human-interest story and the color feature: The former focuses on the emotion of the participants, while the latter focuses on the event or topic. If that event is a parade or march—a tractorcade by the American Agricultural Movement, for instance—the reporter would describe the tractors, of course, and the signs that protested government policy. But the writer also would note what the signs were made of, how they were painted, where they were displayed, what they said, how the spectators responded—and a dozen other details that would enliven an otherwise obtuse story for the print media.

Sometimes a writer is able to combine elements of both approaches. A newspaper reporter in South Dakota was assigned to do a feature story about The Shrine to Music, one of the world's largest collections of musical instruments.

The reporter focused the human interest on the curator, who collected the instruments, recounting how he came to love music and then turned to the instruments from the common clarinet to exotic drums.

The subject matter of a feature will determine the diction, or choice of words, a writer uses to tell a story. If you are writing about opera and the fine arts and are planning to use Latin-based words, such as *allegro* or *a capella*, be sure to clarify them so that every reader will understand. If you are writing about sports, do not exclude readers by using slang such as *roundballer* or *charity stripe*. *Remember, the correct word is the one that communicates.*

The clear and effective word makes your copy vivid in the reader's mind. It expresses your enthusiasm for a feature idea, presents research through facts and quotations, introduces sources who explain newsworthy subjects, focuses on the human situation and, most importantly, holds the reader's interest from lead to wrap-up.

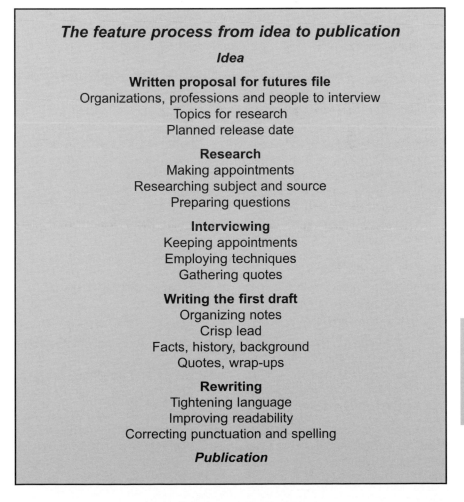

The feature process from idea to publication

Idea

Written proposal for futures file
Organizations, professions and people to interview
Topics for research
Planned release date

Research
Making appointments
Researching subject and source
Preparing questions

Interviewing
Keeping appointments
Employing techniques
Gathering quotes

Writing the first draft
Organizing notes
Crisp lead
Facts, history, background
Quotes, wrap-ups

Rewriting
Tightening language
Improving readability
Correcting punctuation and spelling

Publication

Features

25. How to create an ethics code

Journalists who develop strong writing and reporting skills and who dedicate themselves to the First Amendment owe it to their publishers and readers to be ethical in their coverage.

If you don't care about ethics, you lack the one trait of a successful reporter: *zeal*.

Journalism is hard work. To do it well you have to have a *calling*—a spiritual word that means you will do all it takes to get the story. You'll research, interview, write, edit, revise, invest time and your own and your publisher's money to be accurate and fair, because those ethical traits ensure penetrating coverage.

Your byline is your word, literally. When you give it, you become part of The Fourth Estate, or fourth branch of government. You are a watchdog over the judicial, legislative and executive branches.

At the Greenlee School of Journalism and Communication at Iowa State University, *our first priority is the Fourth Estate*.

That's our motto.

We recognize that along with rights, journalists have responsibilities. They have to be objective, seeing the world as it actually is rather than as they wish it would be. That also means they cannot take gifts or junkets offered by publicists or corporations that lead reporters to see the world as *sources* would like them to see it. *Reporters may not stereotype others. They do not steal words from other writers and pass them off as their own. They have a sacred obligation to defend the Bill of Rights and to inform citizens of the republic so that they can make intelligent choices in the voting booth.*

To remember these and other tenets, you need an ethics code.

Ethics codes enhance reporting in all media. Magazine feature writers rely on them as much as newspaper reporters.

"An ethics code definitely makes me think about my audience," said Meghan Aftosmis, associate researcher for *National Geographic Traveler.* "It reminds me to be responsible and always stand behind what I have written."

"I keep my code in my portfolio," Aftosmis added.

Here's an excerpt:

> Uphold the **freedom of the press**. Put personal beliefs and opinions out of mind and be **objective**. Question everything. Avoid stereotypes in writing. ... Even under stress and deadline pressure, never forget the audience. ... That relationship, like all others, must be based on **respect** and **trust**.

Another journalist, Darin Painter—former editor of *The Post*, the award-winning student newspaper at Ohio University—observed: "Ethics is not an afterthought. You have to be ethical *before* you pen your stories."

Ethics

Reporters must not unduly favor one source over another or stereotype anyone, Painter said. Instead, understand viewpoints. "Quotes have to be accurate. The facts have to be there. You cannot take quotes out of context. If you think, *'This quote is going to benefit me and make me look better,'* then you're not taking your audience into account."

Painter emphasized that journalists should realize "the words that you write and the final appearance of what you write will affect others."

Painter, now a magazine journalist, has adapted his newspaper ethics to his current job as managing editor of *Print Solutions*. In fact, Painter's code played a role in his hiring. "My boss said that doing an ethics code distinguished me from others. I am happy I had to produce one, and it is on my corkboard at work— an updated version."

Here's an excerpt:

> Ethical magazine journalists know more than an audience; they know themselves. By developing strong personal value systems, they can be responsible catalysts of integrity, fairness and excellence—concepts that both co-workers and readers respect and deserve.

Painter's values apply to any assignment in newspaper or magazine journalism. His values renew his zeal. Of course, you can develop similar habits without a code. But having one reminds you of your ethical obligations.

A code should promote high, consistent standards such as fairness to sources, respect for readers and accuracy for editors.

Codes not only welcome good habits, they also warn about bad ones. For instance, reporters must guard against conflict of interest—even the perception of it. They may not take bribes, junkets (free trips) or freebies (gifts) from sources in return for favorable stories. They should pay their own way, too, even while doing restaurant or movie reviews or covering sports or theatrical events. Some newspapers have written policies on this with the general caveat that reporters should accept no gift or ticket, etc., worth more than $25.

Neither should reporters indulge in nonmonetary conflicts of interest, doing stories in which they or their newspaper has a vested interest. That includes things such as writing a negative story about a staff member's landlord because of a strict rental policy or doing a favorable story about an apartment complex owned by the publisher's family. An ethics code will guide reporters through real and perceived conflicts of interests. A code also should warn not to take shortcuts (the shortest being plagiarism); nor should a reporter:

- Invent quotations or quote sources out of context.
- Stereotype others based on race, gender, social class or religion.
- Deceive editors, padding expenses as well as prose.
- Steal company supplies (paper, print cartridges, disks, etc.).

Ethics

A good code should challenge the reporter. Before turning in copy to an editor, the ethical journalist asks:

- Is the manuscript legal, accurate, truthful and responsible?
- Does it enlighten without manipulation?
- Does it address the readers' needs?
- Is it sensitive toward others and their viewpoints?

If the manuscript does not meet such criteria, the reporter has to revise until it does. That kind of work ethic attracts editors and builds a reputation for credibility, the ultimate goal of a code.

Once you know what your code should accomplish, you should create one.

Follow these steps:

Write brief statements about useful reporting habits such as fairness, respect and accuracy. Also compose ones warning about temptation, manipulation and bias.

Assemble your statements in a text document, and revise the wording of each so that all are similar in length and read in a consistent, parallel manner. (Common errors include using the first person, *I*, in some statements and not in others and switching verb case or tense.)

Show a draft of your code to an ace reporter or to your editor or publisher, and request a critique.

Revise again, incorporating suggestions or enhancing content.

Insert your text into the desired format. Many reporters opt for a business format with codes in the same style as their résumés, printing their values on the back of them. Some journalists create brochures or post their codes on the Web. Use the format that best showcases your code.

Include your code in a portfolio. Or hang it on your office wall.

Revisit your code annually and revise it accordingly so that it becomes a living document.

Celebrate and defend your ethics, along with the Bill of Rights, the ethics code of the United States of America.

Ethics